CAREER EXPLORATION

Electrician

by Karen J. Donnelly

Consultant:
Mary M. Germershausen, Director
Systems Technology
National Electrical Contractors Association

CAPSTONE BOOKS
an imprint of Capstone Press
Mankato, Minnesota

Capstone Books are published by Capstone Press
151 Good Counsel Drive, P.O. Box 669, Mankato, Minnesota 56002
http://www.capstone-press.com

Library of Congress Cataloging-in-Publication Data
Donnelly, Karen J.
      Electrician/by Karen J. Donnelly.
      p. cm.—(Career exploration)
      Includes bibliographical references and index.
      Summary: Introduces the career of electrician, discussing educational
requirements, duties, work environment, salary, employment outlook, and possible
future positions.
      ISBN 0-7368-0594-X
      1. Electricians—Vocational guidance—Juvenile literature. [1. Electricians—
Vocational guidance. 2. Vocational guidance.] I. Title. II. Series.
TK159 .D66 2001
621.319'24'023—dc21   00-022446

Editorial Credits
Leah K. Pockrandt, editor; Steve Christensen, cover designer; Kia Bielke, production
      designer and illustrator; Heidi Schoof and Kimberly Danger, photo researchers

Photo Credits
David F. Clobes, cover, 6, 9, 10, 12, 15, 16, 20, 23, 26, 34, 36, 39, 41, 43, 47
National Joint Apprenticeship and Training Committee (NJATC), 33
Shaffer Photography/James L. Shaffer, 28
Unicorn Stock Photos/Travis Evans, 19; Dennis MacDonald, 31

**Special thanks to A.J. Pearson, Executive Director of the National Joint
Apprenticeship and Training Committee, for his assistance with this book.**

      2 3 4 5 6 06 05 04 03 02

Table of Contents

Fast Facts

Career Title	Electrician
O*NET Number	87202A
DOT Cluster (Dictionary of Occupational Titles)	Structural work occupations
DOT Number	824.261-010
GOE Number (Guide for Occupational Exploration)	05.05.05/05.05.10
NOC Number (National Occupational Classification-Canada)	7241/7242/721
Salary Range (U.S. Bureau of Labor Statistics and Human Resources Development Canada, late 1990s figures)	U.S.: $17,628-$52,936 Canada: $14,600-$63,000 (Canadian dollars)
Minimum Educational Requirements	U.S.: apprenticeship or on-the-job training Canada: apprenticeship or on-the-job training
Certification/Licensing Requirements	U.S.: varies by state Canada: varies by province

Subject Knowledge

Computers and electronics; engineering and technology; algebra; design; building and construction; physics; education and training; public safety and security

Personal Abilities/Skills

Use hand tools or machines skillfully; read blueprints and drawings of items to be made or repaired; measure, cut, and work on materials or objects with great precision; use arithmetic and geometry to figure amounts of materials needed, dimensions, and costs; accept responsibility for the accuracy of completed work; use communication skills

Job Outlook

U.S.: average growth
Canada: fair

Personal Interests

Mechanical: interest in applying mechanical principles to practical situations, using machines, hand tools, or techniques

Similar Types of Jobs

Air-conditioning mechanic; cable installer and repairer; electronics mechanic; elevator constructor

Chapter 1

Electrician

Electricians work with electricity. They install, maintain, and repair electrical wiring, equipment, and fixtures. These devices bring electricity to homes, factories, and other buildings.

Types of Electricians

Electricians work as inside wiremen or outside linemen. Inside wiremen mainly work inside buildings. Outside linemen mainly work on power lines.

Inside wiremen connect electrical systems in buildings to outside power lines. They also install, maintain, or repair electrical equipment and circuits inside buildings. The flow of electricity is called electrical current. The circuit is the path that the current follows.

Electricians install, maintain, and repair electrical wiring and fixtures.

Inside wiremen perform much of their work inside. They work on a variety of systems such as fire alarms, burglar alarms, and temperature controls. They also work on telephone, lighting, and power systems. Electricians may install the wiring and outlets for computer systems in office buildings. They also may install wiring in hotels and motels for phones and cable TV. Some inside wiremen also work on electrical lines that connect buildings and power lines.

Outside linemen often work for power companies. Power plants produce the electricity that flows through power lines. Some power lines hang between utility poles located along streets. Other power lines are buried underground.

Outside linemen maintain or repair power lines. Some outside linemen install new power poles and lines. They also may maintain and repair traffic or train signals.

Electricians follow blueprints to see where conduit should be placed.

Blueprints and Codes

Electricians follow blueprints. These detailed plans show where electricians should lay conduit. These rigid metal or PVC pipes protect electrical wiring. PVC is a hard plastic-like material. Wiring is run through the conduit to

Electricians must follow safety guidelines and codes.

provide electric power throughout a building.
Conduit also keeps wiring in place.

Blueprints also show a building's electrical
circuit. The circuit includes lighting fixtures,
wall plug outlets, and switches.

Electricians must follow building codes. These
rules make sure that all electricians follow the
same safety guidelines. Cities, states, and
provinces have different building codes. In the

United States, electricians must also follow the safety guidelines of the National Electrical Code. In Canada, electricians must also follow the Canadian Electrical Code.

Specialty Areas

Most electricians work in the construction industry. These electricians also are called construction electricians. These electricians install the electrical systems that provide power to buildings. They also connect the buildings' wiring to the outside power lines.

Some electricians work in maintenance departments of businesses or factories. These maintenance electricians perform the day-to-day repair of electrical systems. They also may maintain and repair electrical machinery. In Canada, maintenance electricians also are called industrial electricians.

Other electricians are self-employed. These electricians often work for short periods of time on several projects. But they may work on large construction jobs. Self-employed electricians mainly work on home construction. They also may perform smaller jobs such as wire repair in homes.

Chapter 2

Day-to-Day Activities

Electricians' daily activities vary. Different types of electricians perform different duties. Inside wiremen can specialize in two areas. They can be construction electricians or maintenance electricians. Outside wiremen generally work on power lines.

Equipment

Electricians use a variety of tools. They use hand tools such as wire strippers, screwdrivers, and hammers. Other hand tools include socket sets and pliers. Electricians also use power tools such as drills and meters. Electricians use meters to measure voltage. Voltage is the force of an electrical current.

Many inside wiremen are construction electricians.

Outside linemen also use a variety of other equipment. They use shovels to dig holes and ladders to climb utility poles. They use hoists to help them lift heavy objects. Outside linemen also wear rubber gloves and use hot sticks to handle energized lines. They use hot sticks to safely handle wires they cannot touch with their hands.

Electricians must wear safety equipment to prevent injuries. They wear safety glasses and hard hats. Outside linemen also must wear safety belts or harnesses when climbing utility poles.

Construction Electricians at Work

To begin a project, construction electricians study blueprints and code specifications. The job foreman or lead electrician orders the needed materials and tools. Construction electricians check the blueprints to see where the power lines should connect to the building. Blueprints also indicate where to locate the high voltage room or electrical closet inside buildings. The electrical panel is located in this room.

Construction electricians use blueprints to decide where to place the conduit. They prepare conduit by cutting and bending it. Construction

Construction electricians must prepare conduit before they install it.

electricians next install the conduit. They then pull the wires through the conduit.

Construction electricians also install switches and power outlets. Electricians test the circuit to make sure all the parts function properly.

Maintenance Electricians at Work

Maintenance electricians work in a variety of locations. For example, they may work in hospitals.

Outside linemen use bucket trucks to help them repair or replace power lines.

Hospital maintenance electricians maintain hospital circuits. They also must maintain backup systems. These systems supply power to hospital machines if the outside power is cut off.

Some maintenance electricians work in stores or shopping malls. These electricians may work with sound or security systems. They keep all of these systems working properly.

Factories also employ maintenance electricians. These electricians maintain the circuits that supply power to the factory buildings. They also may maintain and repair factory equipment.

Outside Linemen at Work

Outside linemen study blueprints and code specifications to plan new projects. They decide what tools and materials will be needed.

Outside linemen set wooden utility poles in the ground. Linemen must set these poles straight. They use power equipment such as augers to dig utility pole holes. Before digging, linemen must make sure that it will be safe to dig. Dangerous accidents can happen if a lineman breaks an underground gas or water pipe.

Outside linemen also repair and replace power lines. Linemen sometimes use bucket trucks to reach these wires. Bucket trucks have a long metal arm with a telescoping, insulated bucket attached to the end. This bucket can move in several directions. At other times, linemen climb poles to repair power lines.

Outside linemen may inspect insulators to make sure that they are working properly. Insulators are used on outside power lines where the wires touch the poles. Insulators stop the current from moving into the pole and traveling through the wood to the ground. They often are made of ceramic. This hard clay substance blocks the flow of electricity. Linemen may need to replace old or damaged insulators.

Outside linemen also install transformers. These pieces of equipment change the current's voltage. It is easier to transport electricity over long distances at higher voltages. Transformers may be step-up or step-down transformers. Circuits work similar to the water pressure that pushes water through pipes and out of faucets. Water flows from faucets more slowly when the water pressure is low. The force of the electric current is weaker when the voltage is low.

Transformers are connected to outside power lines. Transformers lower the voltage in a power line to 240 volts. This voltage is the standard needed in most home and small business circuits. Linemen need to be able to determine what type of transformers should be used. They remove old transformers before installing new ones.

Outside linemen also install underground wires and conduit. Underground wires and

Outside linemen often install transformers.

conduit are buried in underground trenches. Linemen decide where these long, narrow ditches will be located. Linemen cut and bend the conduit. They also pull the cable through the conduit. Other workers then cover the conduit with concrete and fill in the trench with dirt.

Chapter 3

The Right Candidate

Electricians need a variety of skills and abilities. They should be responsible, patient, and physically fit. They must be able to think quickly. Electricians also must be detail-oriented and precise.

Abilities

Electricians need to understand how electricity works. They must know how to control the flow of electricity safely to avoid fires or electrical shocks.

Electricians must work in a variety of conditions. Some of these conditions may be unpleasant. Construction electricians may have to work in small, cramped spaces. They may work in these spaces for long periods of time.

Electricians also must work in a variety of weather conditions. Buildings at construction sites

Electricians need a variety of skills.

are open to rain, sleet, snow, heat, and humidity. Construction electricians often must perform site work in these conditions.

Outside linemen perform many of their tasks throughout the year. They also must work in a variety of weather conditions.

Electrician jobs often require physical strength. Electricians need to lift and carry equipment and supplies. They also may need to stand for long periods of time. They may work on utility poles, ladders, or scaffolding. Workers stand on these wooden or metal structures when they work on tall buildings. Electricians should not be afraid of heights. Outside linemen also must have good climbing skills.

Electricians should have good eyesight and motor skills. Their work is detailed. They must be able to hold small hand tools steady while they are connecting circuits. They must be able to carefully measure and cut materials.

Electricians need good color vision. They cannot be colorblind. Electricians must be able to tell the difference between different colored wires. The colors indicate how the wires should be connected to the circuits.

Electricians need good eyesight and motor skills.

Skills

Electricians must be able to read blueprints. They use blueprints to help them plan the wiring of a building or placement of utility poles.

Electricians should have good math skills. Some electricians use geometry to plan the layouts that they will follow. This area of math deals with lines, angles, and shapes. Other electricians must determine the amounts and costs of needed materials.

Skills

Workplace Skills   Yes / No

Resources:
Assign use of time . . . . ☑ ☐
Assign use of money . . . . ☐ ☑
Assign use of material and facility resources . . . . ☑ ☐
Assign use of human resources . . . . ☑ ☐

Interpersonal Skills:
Take part as a member of a team . . . . ☑ ☐
Teach others . . . . ☑ ☐
Serve clients/customers . . . . ☑ ☐
Show leadership . . . . ☑ ☐
Work with others to arrive at a decision . . . . ☑ ☐
Work with a variety of people . . . . ☑ ☐

Information:
Acquire and judge information . . . . ☑ ☐
Understand and follow legal requirements . . . . ☑ ☐
Organize and maintain information . . . . ☑ ☐
Understand and communicate information . . . . ☑ ☐
Use computers to process information . . . . ☑ ☐

Systems:
Identify, understand, and work with systems . . . . ☑ ☐
Understand environmental, social, political, economic,
    or business systems . . . . ☑ ☐
Oversee and correct system performance . . . . ☑ ☐
Improve and create systems . . . . ☑ ☐

Technology:
Select technology . . . . ☑ ☐
Apply technology to task . . . . ☑ ☐
Maintain and troubleshoot technology . . . . ☑ ☐

Foundation Skills

Basic Skills:
Read . . . . ☑ ☐
Write . . . . ☑ ☐
Do arithmetic and math . . . . ☑ ☐
Speak and listen . . . . ☑ ☐

Thinking Skills:
Learn . . . . ☑ ☐
Reason . . . . ☑ ☐
Think creatively . . . . ☑ ☐
Make decisions . . . . ☑ ☐
Solve problems . . . . ☑ ☐

Personal Qualities:
Take individual responsibility . . . . ☑ ☐
Have self-esteem and self-management . . . . ☑ ☐
Be sociable . . . . ☑ ☐
Be fair, honest, and sincere . . . . ☑ ☐

Construction electricians should be able to envision what projects will look like. They must understand how rooms in houses and other buildings will be used. This helps them install switches and wall outlets in the best places.

Electricians must be responsible and have good judgment. They must solve problems quickly. They also must be willing to accept responsibility for the accuracy of their work.

Electricians need good communication skills. They talk with employers, building owners, and other construction workers. They must give and understand both written and spoken instructions.

Electricians must be able to work as part of a team. For example, they may work with carpenters, masons, and other construction workers to complete projects. Electricians must complete their work on time to keep projects on schedule.

Chapter 4

Preparing for the Career

Electricians need training to perform their jobs. Some electricians attend a community college or vocational school. Some receive training in an apprenticeship program.

High School Education

High school students who want to become electricians should take a variety of classes. They should study math, science, and electronics. Students learn how to solve complex math problems in algebra classes. They learn how electricity works in physics classes. Students learn how to apply this knowledge in electronics classes.

Electricians need training to perform their jobs.

Students may learn how electrical machines work in industrial arts classes.

Students interested in becoming electricians may take drafting and industrial arts classes. Students learn how to make mechanical drawings and read blueprints in drafting classes. They learn how electrical machines work in industrial arts classes. They may even learn how to wire electrical circuits in these classes.

Students may benefit from computer classes. They learn how to use computers and different programs in these classes. Computers often are used to control temperatures, elevators, and lighting.

Many high schools also offer programs that allow students to work with employers. Students interested in becoming electricians can gain experience as they work in these programs.

Apprenticeship Programs

Most electricians learn the skills needed for their jobs through apprenticeship programs. The National Electrical Contractors Association (NECA) and International Brotherhood of Electrical Workers (IBEW) operate joint apprenticeship programs. The IBEW is a union. Many electricians belong to unions. These labor organizations negotiate electricians' pay rates, benefits, and working conditions. To negotiate, two or more individuals or groups discuss items until they reach an agreement.

Apprenticeship programs usually last four or five years. Programs include classroom instruction and on-the-job training. Apprentices are paid during training. Experienced journeyman electricians supervise the apprentices' on-the-job training. A journeyman is a person who has completed an apprenticeship.

Typical IBEW/NECA apprenticeship programs include at least 180 hours of classroom instruction each year. Apprentices study electrical theory, blueprint reading, electronics, and math. They learn safety requirements and the National Electrical Code. Some apprentices receive special training in communications and alarm systems or welding.

Apprenticeship programs also include 8,000 hours of on-the-job training. Apprentices first perform basic jobs such as drilling holes and bending conduit. They perform more complex jobs as they gain experience. Apprentices install, connect, and test equipment such as wiring, outlets, and switches. They also learn to set up and draw diagrams for electrical systems.

Other Training

Some people who want to be electricians attend a community college or vocational or technical school. Students at these schools study the same subjects as apprentices do.

Students earn an associate's degree at these schools. Most students complete an associate's degree in two years. Some of these students also

Some electrician apprentices learn how to weld.

complete an apprenticeship program in addition
to their degree.

Licensing and Certification
Most states require electricians to be licensed.
Licensing requirements vary according to area
or state. Most electricians must pass an exam.
This test covers local electrical codes, electrical
theory, and the National Electrical Code.

In Canada, most maintenance electricians are certified. To obtain trade certification, electricians must pass an exam. Electricians also must study the Canadian Electrical Code to be certified. Some provinces require electricians to be certified. These provinces are Nova Scotia, Prince Edward Island, New Brunswick, Quebec, Ontario, Manitoba, Saskatchewan, and Alberta.

In Canada, many construction electricians are certified. Prince Edward Island is the only province that requires certification.

Some electricians in Canada obtain further certification. These electricians obtain the Red Seal. This trade certification allows electricians to work in different provinces.

In Canada, linemen may need provincial trade certification. The certification requirements vary in each province.

Continuing Education

Licensed electricians should continue their education throughout their career. They should upgrade their skills every year. This ensures that they know the most current information and electrical procedures. They must keep up with changes in the National Electrical Code.

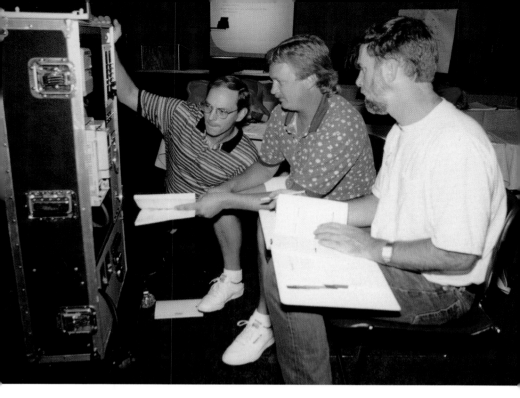

Electricians need to learn about new technology.

Electricians must continue to learn about new technology. Computers will continue to change the way electrical systems are controlled. Electricians must understand how the newest systems work. Electricians often take courses that are offered by their employers or unions.

Some states and provinces require electricians to take a set amount of continuing education each year. This amount varies depending on state or province.

Chapter 5

The Market

Electricians have many job opportunities. But the job outlook for electricians can vary with the economy. Electricians will be needed as new buildings are built and old ones are restored. They also will be needed to replace electricians who leave the field.

Salary

Electricians' salaries depend on several factors. Experienced electricians usually earn the highest salaries. Electricians with special skills also may earn more money. Electricians who are supervisors earn more money because they have greater responsibilities.

Salaries also vary depending on location. Electricians in larger cities may earn more money than electricians in rural areas.

Electricians have many job opportunities.

Electricians will be needed to maintain equipment.

Apprentices earn the least because they are still learning the job. Apprentices usually start at about 50 percent of the journeyman pay rate.

In the United States, most electricians earn between $17,628 and $52,936 per year. The average annual salary for electricians is $32,240.

In Canada, most electricians earn between $14,600 and $63,000 per year. Line electricians earn between $14,600 and $54,800 per year. The average annual salary for a lineman is

$36,300. Construction electricians earn between $17,900 and $54,700 per year. The average annual salary for construction electricians is $37,300.

Maintenance electricians in Canada earn between $29,100 and $63,000. The average annual salary for maintenance electricians is $45,100. The Human Resources Development Canada groups the salaries of maintenance electricians with other workers. These workers include specialized electricians who have advanced training. The Human Resources Development Canada is a government agency that gathers and reviews career information.

Benefits

Electricians often receive benefits in addition to salaries. For most electricians, these benefits include life insurance and retirement programs. Maintenance electricians also often receive paid vacations, sick leave, and medical insurance. Electricians may receive benefits from a union or an employer.

Electricians also may participate in retirement programs or pension plans. A pension is an amount of money paid regularly to a retired person. Electricians put money in these programs while they work. They receive the money after they retire.

Job Outlook
In the United States, the electrician field is expected to have average growth. An increased demand for electricians may create additional job openings. But employment is expected to have slower than average growth. Additional construction may not always create new jobs.

In Canada, the job market for electricians is expected to have fair growth. The job outlook for maintenance electricians is good. These electricians will be needed as companies become more dependent upon machines. Electricians will be needed to maintain such equipment. But the job outlook for linemen and construction electricians is poor. The demand for these jobs depends upon the weather and the economy.

The job outlook for electricians is best when the economy is good. More jobs are available for electricians when more new buildings are being built. Fewer buildings are built when the economy is poor. Even maintenance electricians may be laid off in a poor economy when employers try to cut costs.

The job outlook for maintenance electricians is good.

Job opportunities for electricians vary by region, state, and province. The market will be best where the local economy is strongest. One area of a country may have a large number of electricians. But another area may have a shortage of electricians.

New technologies also will increase the need for electricians. New buildings may be wired to make it easier to install computers and other communications equipment. More factories will use robots and other automated systems. These systems will need to be installed and maintained by electricians.

Advancement Opportunities
Electricians may advance as they gain more training and experience. They also may advance when they learn special skills. Experienced electricians may become supervisors.

Some electricians start their own businesses. These electricians may work for building contractors. These people build or remodel houses and other buildings. Companies also may hire independent electricians to work on special projects. The companies' electricians may not be trained for such projects.

In the United States, many self-employed electricians have master electrician status. They achieve this by completing additional classes and passing an exam. The exam may contain written and practical sections. Electricians demonstrate their skills during practical exams. Master electrician requirements vary with each state.

Related Careers
People interested in electrical systems have a variety of career options. Some people become

Some experienced electricians become supervisors.

air conditioning mechanics. These skilled workers service air conditioning systems. Other people may install and repair TV cable. Still others may become elevator constructors. These individuals build or repair elevators in buildings.

Electricians provide an important service to many people. Electricians will be needed to keep electrical systems working as technology advances in the future.

Words to Know

apprentice (uh-PREN-tiss)—a person who learns a job by working with an experienced worker

circuit (SUR-kit)—the complete path of an electrical current

conduit (KON-doo-it)—a pipe or tube that protects electrical wires

insulator (IN-suh-late-or)—a material that blocks an electrical current

journeyman (JUR-nee-man)—a worker who has learned a job; an experienced electrician is a journeyman.

transformer (transs-FOR-mur)—a device that changes the voltage of an electrical current

voltage (VOHL-tij)—the force of an electrical current; voltage is measured in volts.

To Learn More

Careers in Focus: Construction. 2d ed.
  Chicago: Ferguson Publishing, 1999.

Cosgrove, Holli, ed. *Career Discovery
  Encyclopedia.* Vol. 3. 4th ed. Chicago:
  Ferguson Publishing, 2000.

**Farr, J. Michael, and LaVerne L. Ludden,
  eds.** *Best Jobs for the 21st Century.*
  Indianapolis: JIST Works, 1999.

Wood, Robert B. *Opportunities in Electrical
  Trades.* VGM Opportunities. Lincolnwood,
  Ill.: VGM Career Horizons, 1997.

*Young People's Occupational Outlook
  Handbook.* 2d ed. Indianapolis: JIST Works,
  1999.

Useful Addresses

Electrical Construction Association
370 York Boulevard
Suite 102
Hamilton, ON L8R 3L1
Canada

**International Brotherhood of Electrical
   Workers**
1125 15th Street NW
Washington, DC 20005

National Electrical Contractors Association
3 Bethesda Metro Center
Suite 1100
Bethesda, MD 20814

National Electrical Safety Foundation
1300 North 17th Street
Suite 1847
Rosslyn, VA 22209

45

Internet Sites

International Brotherhood of Electrical Workers (IBEW)
http://www.ibew.org

Job Futures–Electricians (Except Industrial and Power Systems)
http://www.jobfutures.ca/jobfutures/noc/ 7241.html

National Electrical Contractors Association (NECA)
http://www.necanet.org

National Joint Apprenticeship and Training Committee (NJATC)
http://www.njatc.org

Occupational Outlook Handbook– Electricians
http://stats.bls.gov/oco/ocos206.htm

Index